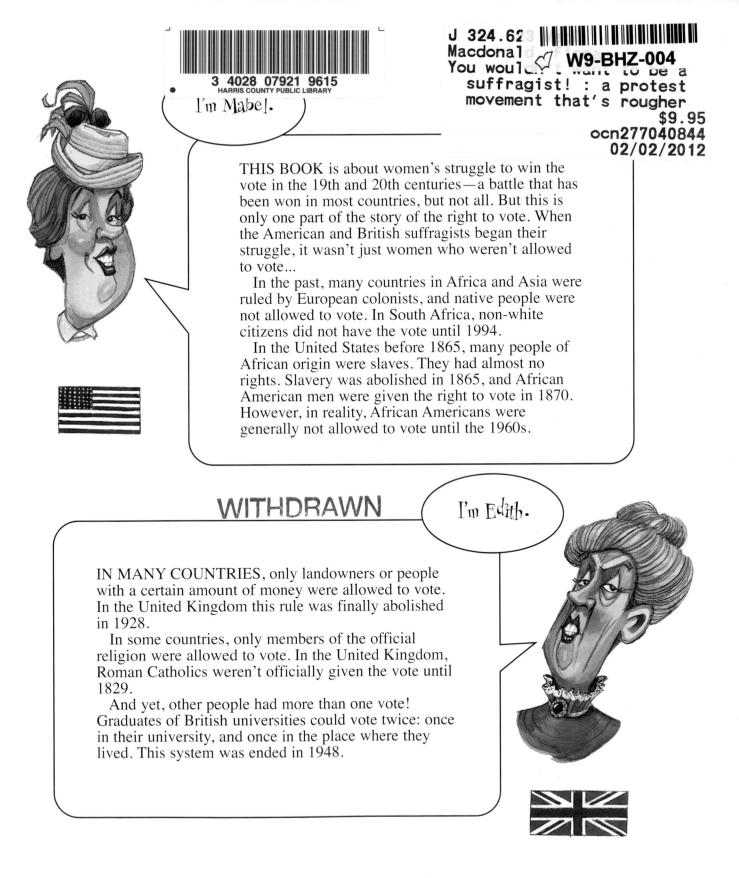

I'm Mabel.

THIS BOOK is about women's struggle to win the vote in the 19th and 20th centuries—a battle that has been won in most countries, but not all. But this is only one part of the story of the right to vote. When the American and British suffragists began their struggle, it wasn't just women who weren't allowed to vote...

In the past, many countries in Africa and Asia were ruled by European colonists, and native people were not allowed to vote. In South Africa, non-white citizens did not have the vote until 1994.

In the United States before 1865, many people of African origin were slaves. They had almost no rights. Slavery was abolished in 1865, and African American men were given the right to vote in 1870. However, in reality, African Americans were generally not allowed to vote until the 1960s.

I'm Edith.

IN MANY COUNTRIES, only landowners or people with a certain amount of money were allowed to vote. In the United Kingdom this rule was finally abolished in 1928.

In some countries, only members of the official religion were allowed to vote. In the United Kingdom, Roman Catholics weren't officially given the vote until 1829.

And yet, other people had more than one vote! Graduates of British universities could vote twice: once in their university, and once in the place where they lived. This system was ended in 1948.

Author:
Fiona Macdonald studied history at
Cambridge University, and at the University of East
Anglia, both in England. She has taught in schools,
in universities, and in adult education. She is the
author of numerous books for children on
historical topics.

Artist:
David Antram was born in Brighton, England,
in 1958. He studied at Eastbourne College of Art
and then worked in advertising for fifteen years
before becoming a full-time artist. He has
illustrated many children's nonfiction books.

Series creator:
David Salariya was born in Dundee, Scotland.
He has illustrated a wide range of books and has
created and designed many new series for
publishers in the UK and overseas. He established
The Salariya Book Company in 1989. He lives in
Brighton with his wife, illustrator Shirley Willis,
and their son Jonathan.

Editors: **Tanya Kant, Stephen Haynes**

Editorial Assistant: **Mark Williams**

© The Salariya Book Company Ltd MMVIII
No part of this publication may be reproduced in whole or in
part, or stored in a retrieval system, or transmitted in any form or
by any means, electronic, mechanical, photocopying, recording,
or otherwise, without written permission of the publisher. For
information regarding permission, write to the copyright holder.

Published in Great Britain in 2008 by
The Salariya Book Company Ltd
25 Marlborough Place, Brighton BN1 1UB

ISBN-13: 978-0-531-20701-7 (lib. bdg.) 978-0-531-21911-9 (pbk.)
ISBN-10: 0-531-20701-3 (lib. bdg.) 0-531-21911-9 (pbk.)

All rights reserved.
Published in 2009 in the United States
by Franklin Watts
An imprint of Scholastic Inc.
Published simultaneously in Canada.

A CIP catalog record for this book is available
from the Library of Congress.

Printed and bound in China.
Printed on paper from sustainable sources.

SCHOLASTIC, FRANKLIN WATTS, and associated logos are
trademarks and/or registered trademarks of Scholastic Inc.

You Wouldn't Want to Be a Suffragist!

Written by
Fiona Macdonald

Illustrated by
David Antram

Created and designed by
David Salariya

A Protest Movement That's Rougher Than You Expected

Franklin Watts®

An Imprint of Scholastic Inc.

NEW YORK • TORONTO • LONDON • AUCKLAND • SYDNEY

MEXICO CITY • NEW DELHI • HONG KONG

DANBURY, CONNECTICUT

Contents

Introduction

It's 1920, and you're a fashionable young American woman. You lead a pretty independent life, but your feisty Great-Aunt Edith, visiting from Britain, remembers when things were not so easy:

"Don't ignore that poster, my girl! People have fought and died to win the vote. And now, at last, we British and American women have got it!

"Since 1918, British women have had the freedom to vote. And this year, American women like you have finally won the vote! But things were very different when I was young—30, 40, 50 years ago. My friends and I wanted to vote and take part in politics, but the men in power would not take us seriously.

"It was just the same here in the United States. My American cousin Mabel used to write me with news about how she and other suffragists were fighting to get the vote. That's what they called the campaigners in America: 'suffragists.' In Britain we were often called 'suffragettes.'*

"We had such a struggle! You should be glad you don't have to do it. But believe me, my dear, it was well worth it!"

*"Suffrage" means "the right to vote."

VOTE for

Great-Aunt Edith

Not Equal!

Great-Aunt Edith begins her story:

"**M**en have been able to vote since Ancient Greek times,* but we women have been banned. Why? Because men would not let us! They claimed that women were weak and not as intelligent as men.

"Women have been demanding equality—and the right to vote—for over a hundred years. One of the first was English writer Mary Wollstonecraft. In 1792, her book, *A Vindication of the Rights of Woman*, called for women to be seen as men's partners, not their slaves. I think she was right; don't you?'

* but only if they were free citizens—slaves and foreigners couldn't vote.

FREE SPIRIT. As a lone parent, Mary worked hard to support herself and her young daughter. She wrote books and newspaper articles, ran a home, and helped her many friends. She was a bold, original thinker who dared to question the way society was organized. For all of her short life (1759–1797), she tried to be independent and free from men's control.

6

MEN—and many women—were shocked by Mary Wollstonecraft's passionate, angry writing. They called her wild and wicked—"a hyena in petticoats."

Rights? What Rights?

Edith's American cousin Mabel takes up the story:

"In the States, too, we've had to fight for our rights. It began in the 1840s. Women campaigning to end slavery also began to demand fair treatment for themselves. They wanted everyone—black or white, male or female—to be equal and free.

"Most women in America had no right to vote, take part in government, own property, or have a good education. So, in 1848, Lucretia Mott and Elizabeth Cady Stanton organized the first-ever Women's Convention at Seneca Falls, New York—to demand equality."

Seneca Falls, 1848

MANY SKILLED WOMEN joined the campaign. Elizabeth Cady Stanton was a great writer and researcher. Susan B. Anthony was a rousing speaker. Lucy Stone published a women's-rights newspaper. Lucretia Mott was a Quaker minister. Julia Ward Howe wrote poems, including the patriotic "Battle Hymn of the Republic."

Elizabeth Cady Stanton 1815–1902

Lucy Stone 1818–1893

Susan B. Anthony 1820–1906

Lucretia Mott 1793–1880

Julia Ward Howe 1819–1910

Even the clothes on your back belong to your husband! In some states, even your children!

Shame!

Shocking!

Equal rights? That gets my vote!

SUPPORT FROM FREED SLAVES. Antislavery campaigner Frederick Douglass came to the 1848 convention to support women's calls for equality. In 1851, preacher Sojourner Truth proudly claimed that women were as strong and reliable as men: "Look at me! Look at my arm! I have plowed and planted, and gathered into barns, and no man could do better than me!"

Sojourner Truth 1797–1883

AT SENECA FALLS, 68 women and 32 men signed the Declaration of Sentiments. It proclaimed: "All men and women are created equal" and demanded new laws that would treat American women the same as men.

Frederick Douglass 1818–1895

9

Get Noticed!

Cousin Mabel continues:

"The Seneca Falls Convention definitely inspired women to try to win the right to vote. Campaigning was tough and exhausting, but the suffragists' vision of a better, more equal future drove them on. There were many ways to help the cause. Women who stayed at home, taking care of their families, raised funds to support the movement. Others traveled across the United States, making speeches, holding meetings, and recruiting new supporters."

This speech will really make them sit up!

SUSAN B. ANTHONY (right) was born to a Quaker family who believed in educating girls. She became a teacher and used her free time to fight against slavery. She decided not to marry, because she wanted independence and the freedom to campaign. She traveled all over the United States, making stirring speeches and organizing demonstrations. She wrote letters to many powerful men, demanding women's right to vote.

ELIZABETH CADY (left) was very intelligent, but because she was female, she was not given the opportunity to go to college. She married antislavery campaigner Henry Stanton. While taking care of their seven children, she found time to write books and to compose speeches for her friend Susan B. Anthony. Together they campaigned for women's rights for over 50 years.

Handy Hint

Avoid ridicule! Women at this time wore tight, restricting clothes. Amelia Bloomer wanted the right to dress more comfortably. But her "bloomer" pants were greeted with laughter.

BE DISRUPTIVE!
In 1876, protesters at the United States Centennial (hundredth anniversary) celebrations in Philadelphia interrupted official speeches and presented a Declaration of Rights for Women to the vice president of the United States.

Get Organized! Advertise!

Mabel and Edith take up the story together:

"If you were a campaigner in the United States or Britain, how could you win more support for your cause? We'll tell you what those determined 19th-century women did. On both sides of the Atlantic, they did the same things. They got organized and they advertised! They formed committees. They collected signatures for petitions. They lobbied politicians. They put up posters and handed out badges. They set up groups in factories, churches, and anywhere else that women gathered together."

NOTHING LESS WILL DO!
In 1870, following the abolition of slavery, the U.S. gave the vote to black men. Suffragists were furious that women hadn't gotten the same rights. They demanded "their rights and nothing less!"

In the UK:

1840s: Protesters called Chartists march to demand equal rights and the vote.
1867: The Women's Suffrage Committee in Manchester starts a monster petition.
1897: Local committees link up in a National Union of Women's Suffrage Societies. Now we're getting powerful!

In the U.S.:

1861–1865: Women stop campaigning so that they can nurse injured troops during the Civil War. They win gratitude—but not the vote.
1869: The American Woman Suffrage Association is set up to campaign state by state. The National Woman Suffrage Association is formed with the goal of changing the U.S. Constitution.
1890: The two groups join to form the National American Woman Suffrage Association.

Did you call us the WEAKER sex?

Slowly, step by step, we'll succeed!

We demand votes – NOW!

AWSA

NWSA

12

Handy Hint

Set up a club to discuss new ideas like winning the right to vote. The first women's club was founded in the U.S. in 1868. Soon there were hundreds.

VOTES FOR WOMEN

"Votes for Women" badge

VOTES FOR WOMEN

DRINK? NO! VOTES? YES! In 1874, the Women's Christian Temperance Union was set up in the U.S. to protest against alcohol abuse. Women now believed that they could change and improve society—which was all the more reason for them to have the vote.

Metal badge with portrait of campaign heroine Susan B. Anthony

Yellow roses (and sunflowers) were campaign symbols.

Beware the demon drink!

GOLD OR YELLOW was the symbolic color worn by U.S. campaigners. Their British sisters wore purple, white, and green.

13

Deeds, Not Words!

Great-Aunt Edith again:

"Despite the hard work of some very dedicated people, by 1900, British women still didn't have the vote. Some were becoming desperate. 'How much has 50 years of campaigning achieved? We want results now! And we'll break the law if that's what it takes!'

"In Britain, the suffragists were led by Mrs. Emmeline Pankhurst, the widow of a lawyer who had supported equal rights. In 1903 she founded a radical new organization: the Women's Social and Political Union. It planned to take direct action to win votes for women. Its slogan was: 'Deeds, not words!' And some of the actions they took were pretty extreme...."

Chaining themselves to park railings

Breaking shop windows

Setting mailboxes on fire

Powerful, Passionate Pankhursts

Emmeline Pankhurst was a brave, inspiring leader. The many followers she attracted became known as "suffragettes." Her husband Richard was a lawyer who worked for women's rights. Their two daughters were just as active. Christabel disrupted a Liberal Party meeting in 1905, demanding votes for women. Sylvia designed posters, banners, and badges.

Richard   *Emmeline*

14

Sending a note—on a cow—to the prime minister

Smash!

VOTES FOR WOMEN

Handy Hint

Don't give up! Women in some countries have already won the right to vote. New Zealand was the first, in 1893.

I say!

Digging up golf courses

Burning down railway stations and churches

Knocking off policemen's helmets

Christabel

Sylvia

Blimey!

15

Go to Prison!

Great-Aunt Edith continues:

"By breaking the law, Mrs. Pankhurst and the suffragists knew that they ran the risk of punishment. And punished they were, over and over again. Each time they took part in a violent protest, they were arrested, put on trial, found guilty, and sent to prison. There they were treated harshly. The British government hoped that this would stop them from protesting again.

"Many people admired the suffragists—I know I did! But others felt that if women behaved like criminals, they could not be trusted as equal citizens —or as voters."

LOOK OUT FOR SPIES! The British police are using some of the world's first long-distance cameras to take secret pictures of suffragette protesters. So wear a big hat or a fashionable veil to hide your face.

Prepare for Prison!

BE BRAVE! You'll be handled roughly when you're arrested.

BRRR! UGH! You'll be searched and bathed, and then dressed in a scratchy prison uniform.

TOUGHEN UP! Prison guards and female warders will treat you like a criminal.

POOR FOOD. You'll get only bread and water. Chances are you'll get sick.

LONG NIGHTS. Lights go out at 8:00 p.m. After that you're not allowed to speak until morning.

Imprisoned for fighting for my freedom–where's the justice in that?

Handy Hint

Make new friends in prison. You'll meet suffragists of all ages from many different places.

WEAR YOUR PIN WITH PRIDE. British campaigner Sylvia Pankhurst designs a pin (right) that looks like the iron gates of Holloway Prison, where suffragists are locked up. American protesters wear "Jailed for Freedom" pins.

Torture and Tragedy

More from Great-Aunt Edith:

"Their violent protests were not working, so the suffragists decided to try a new tactic. Now, instead of attacking public property, they planned to risk their own well-being—and even their lives! When they were imprisoned, they vowed, they'd go on hunger strikes. They hoped this would force the government to give in to their demands, rather than see them starve to death.

"Millicent Garrett Fawcett, a wise, experienced campaigner, continued to lead lawful, old-fashioned protests. But these peaceful protests were ignored."

CAT AND MOUSE

Angered by the suffragists' tactics, the British government passed a new law. Suffragists who went on hunger strikes were set free until they were strong and healthy again. Then they were arrested and sent back to prison. Suffragists called this law the "Cat and Mouse Act."

Whoa!

She could have killed me too!

DEATH DIVE. In 1913, suffragist Emily Davison ran out in front of the king of England's horse at the Derby, the most important race of the year. She was knocked down by the horse and died a few days later. A suffragist pin was found on her jacket. Was she mad, or a heroine? Or was her death a tragic accident? People could not agree.

Thump!

THE CAT AND MOUSE ACT
PASSED BY A LIBERAL GOVERNMENT

THE LIBERAL CAT!
ELECTORS VOTE AGAINST HIM!
KEEP THE LIBERAL OUT!

A poster protesting against the "Cat and Mouse Act"

PRISON DOCTORS force-fed hunger-strikers by pouring liquid food down a tube through their noses and into their stomachs. The doctors said this was done to save the protesters' lives. The suffragists said it was torture.

Keep the blasted woman still, can't you?

Handy Hint

Keep your spirits up! Dame Ethel Smyth has composed a song for suffragist prisoners to sing.

"Shout, shout, up with your song!"

It's for your own good, love.

No surrender... no surrender...

Look West!

Cousin Mabel takes up the story:

"American suffragists were making better progress at this time. We faced a setback in 1875, when the Supreme Court declared that women—although citizens like men—did not have the same rights. But our campaigns finally got results when men began to realize how strong and capable women could be. Way out West, women built homes, plowed fields, reared livestock, and defended new communities. By 1896, Wyoming, Utah, Idaho, and Colorado had given votes to women. By 1914, Washington, California, Oregon, Kansas, Arizona, Nevada, Montana, and the Alaska Territory had followed suit."

"THE AWAKENING"
This suffragist poster advocated that eastern states should give votes to women—as many western states and territories had already done.

So–what do you say to that?

WOMAN POWER. Gradually, women got to vote in local elections. Male candidates had to listen to them—and their demands for equal rights.

Get Together!

Cousin Mabel continues:

"When women living in the eastern states saw what their sisters out West had achieved, they were inspired to fight for the vote too. In 1890, the two main suffragist organizations united (see page 12). This gave them renewed strength. In 1913, more than 20,000 suffragists marched through the streets of New York City. In the city's 1915 suffragist parade, there were 40,000 marchers. By 1917, New York's women finally had the vote."

HOW LONG MUST WOMEN WAIT FOR LIBERTY?

MR. PRESIDENT WHAT WILL YOU DO FOR WOMEN'S SUFFRAGE?

PICKET LINE. By 1917, many women in the U.S. still didn't have the right to vote. Suffragists decided to picket the president at the White House in Washington, D.C.

SUFFRAGE PARADES in New York and Washington, D.C., were led by a young woman dressed as the Herald of Liberty, riding an impressive white horse.

Forward into Light!

THE PICKETERS were imprisoned and went on hunger strikes. Picket organizer Alice Paul was put in solitary confinement, and the authorities tried to prove she was insane, or "mad," as they called her.

Handy Hint

Be patriotic! Think of the Statue of Liberty as a suffragist symbol— she's a woman, after all!

TRAGIC HEROINE. The rider on the white horse was Inez Milholland (later Inez Milholland Boissevain), a lawyer and writer. She gave lectures and took part in protests throughout the United States, despite being seriously ill. In 1916 she collapsed from exhaustion and died five weeks later. She was only 30 years old.

INEZ MILHOLLAND BOISSEVAIN

WHO DIED FOR THE FREEDOM OF WOMEN

War Effort

Mabel and Edith remember the Great War: *

"The Great War lasted four terrible years, from 1914 to 1918. This was no time for protests—patriotic duty came first! We women in Britain and the United States called off our suffrage campaigns. Instead, we joined in the war effort, doing all we could to help our countries and our men fighting overseas. We worked as nurses, as women had done in many wars before. But for the first time, we also took on many jobs that were usually done by men. To everyone's surprise— except ours, of course—we proved that we're strong, hardworking, trustworthy, clever, and quick-thinking. Now everyone respected us!"

* *later called World War I*

Who says engineering is harder than sewing?

Next stop: equality!

WE CAN DO IT!
In wartime, women worked as firefighters, farmhands, engineers, and builders; and as drivers and guards on buses, trains, and trams.

WOMEN NURSES traveled to the front line, right where the fighting was happening. They showed great courage, caring for soldiers in battlefield hospitals and driving ambulances through gunfire to rescue the wounded.

Whimper!

Handy Hint

Hide your grief at seeing so many fine men die. The survivors need you to be strong.

Chin up, old girl!

MILLIONS OF MEN died in the war, leaving their families all alone. War widows had to look for work to pay for food and housing.

YOUNG, EDUCATED WOMEN took over professional men's jobs, becoming doctors, lawyers, and professors. Now everyone could see that women are as intelligent as men!

25

Victory!

Edith:

"We worked so hard during the war that our claims could no longer be ignored. In 1918, the British  Parliament gave the vote to British women age 30 or over. This isn't quite equality—men can vote at 21—but never fear, we're working on that!"

Mabel:

 "The law has been changed in the United States, too. Thanks to the 19th Amendment, added to the Constitution in 1920, all American women can vote. It's victory! Our long struggle is over!"

Success!

We did it!

Well worth the effort, I say!

DO YOUR DUTY! Vote wisely and you'll be rewarded. In 1928, British women over 21 will get the vote, just like men.

Ballot box

Ballot

A LIFE IN POLITICS. The right to vote is just one part of women's equality. Now we can also take part in mainstream politics right alongside men. We can hand out leaflets, go on marches, raise funds, sit on committees, and run for election as members of Congress or Parliament. We're equal, and we have a lot to say!

Madam Speaker...

What Happened Next?

1890–1899   1900–1909   1910–1919   1920–1929   1930–1939

Women in Britain and the United States were not alone in campaigning for the vote. Capable, confident women in many countries worldwide also demanded the right to take part in politics. Their success depended on winning support from male politicians and from religious leaders and traditional elders in each nation.

Gradually, a woman's right to vote has spread around the world. Today, it is almost, but not quite, universal. What would Great-Aunt Edith and Cousin Mabel have to say about that?

THIS MAP gives a general idea of when different countries gave women the same voting rights as men.

PIONEER POLITICIANS. There have been many female politicians since women won the right to vote. India, Sri Lanka, Germany, Israel, the Philippines, Norway, Argentina, Pakistan, and many other nations have all had women heads of government or party leaders. In 1979, Margaret Thatcher (left) became Britain's first woman prime minister. She served until 1990. Barbara Jordan (right) was the first African American woman from a southern state to be elected to the U.S. House of Representatives. She served from 1973 to 1979.

28

1940–1949 *1950–1959* *1960–1969* *1970–1979* *1980–1989* *1990–1999* *2000–2009*

Handy Hint

Use your vote! It's too valuable to ignore. With it, you can change the world!

SOME COUNTRIES gave the vote only to white women at first. Other countries had different age requirements for men and women. In some countries, even when women had the right to vote, they didn't always have the right to run for election.

TO FIND OUT MORE about the history of voting in your country, look at up-to-date textbooks and the Internet.

IN 1893, NEW ZEALAND became the first country to give women equal rights.

Glossary

Ballot An official form for voting. It has a list of candidates printed on it, and voters put a mark next to the name of the candidate they want to elect.

Ballot box An official box in which voters put their ballots when they vote. The ballots are locked in the box until it is time for them to be counted.

Campaign To work in an organized way toward a particular social or political goal.

Chartists Members of an English organization (1838–1848) that demanded new laws, including allowing all English men—not just landowners and men with property—to vote.

Colonist A person who settles in another country but is still loyal to his or her home country.

Committee A group of people who meet together to organize something, such as a political campaign.

Equality Treating people fairly, whatever their gender, age, nationality, skin color, or religion.

Great War A name that was often used for World War I (1914–1918), especially before the beginning of World War II (1939–1945).

Hunger strike A protest in which the protester refuses to eat or drink until their demands are met.

Liberal In favor of progress and political reform.

Liberal Party A British political party (1859–1988). Until the 1920s it was one of the two main parties in Britain, and was often in power.

Lobby To meet with politicians and try to persuade them to change the law.

Patriotic Having devotion to and expressing support for one's own country.

Petition A document, signed by a large number of people, that demands a change in the law.

Picket line A line of protesters who try to prevent people from getting into a particular place unless their demands are met.

Quaker A member of the Religious Society of Friends, a Christian group that believes in pacifism (not going to war) and equality.

Solitary confinement A form of imprisonment in which the prisoner is kept alone and is not allowed to meet or speak to anyone.

Speaker The chairperson of the British House of Commons or the U.S. House of Representatives.

Suffrage The right to vote.

Suffragette The nickname given to British women who campaigned for the right to vote.

Suffragist The name preferred by American women who campaigned for the right to vote; also, a member of the National Union of Women's Suffrage Societies in the UK.

Temperance movement A group of people who campaigned against drinking alcohol.

Warder A prison officer.

Index